Smile! What do you … s, and teeth. Teeth help … ur food and cut it up into smaller lumps.

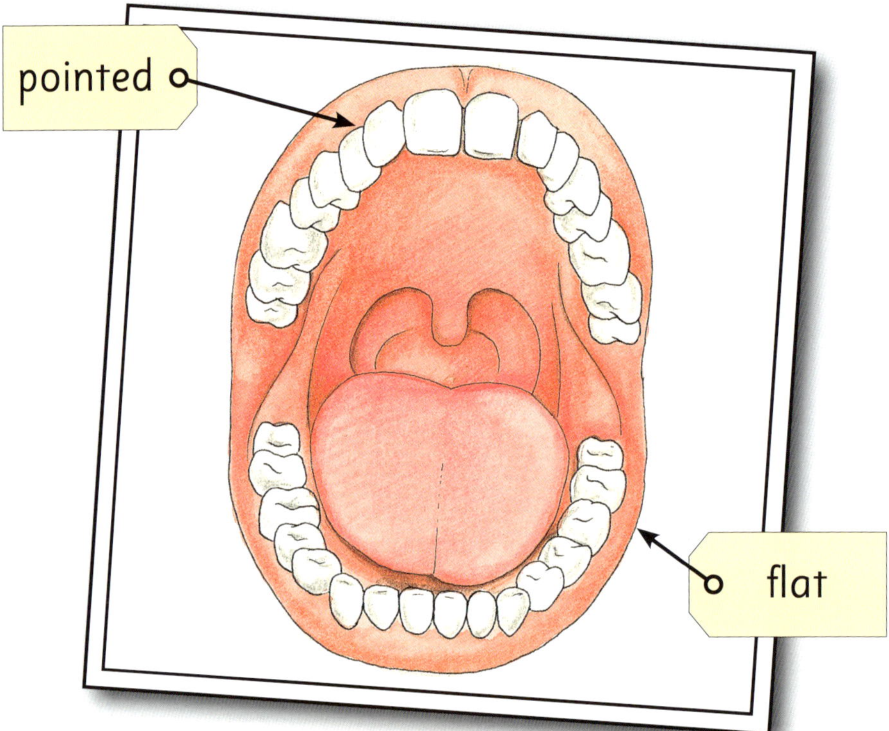

Different shaped teeth have different jobs. Some are shaped like spades and we use them to bite into food. Some are sharp and pointed, so as to shred the lumps of food into smaller bits. Then there are wide, flat teeth at the back of the mouth, which mash the food into a pulp.

When we are born, we have no teeth that can be seen yet. The teeth are all hidden under our gums. When they start to develop, they can make the gums sore. This is called teething.

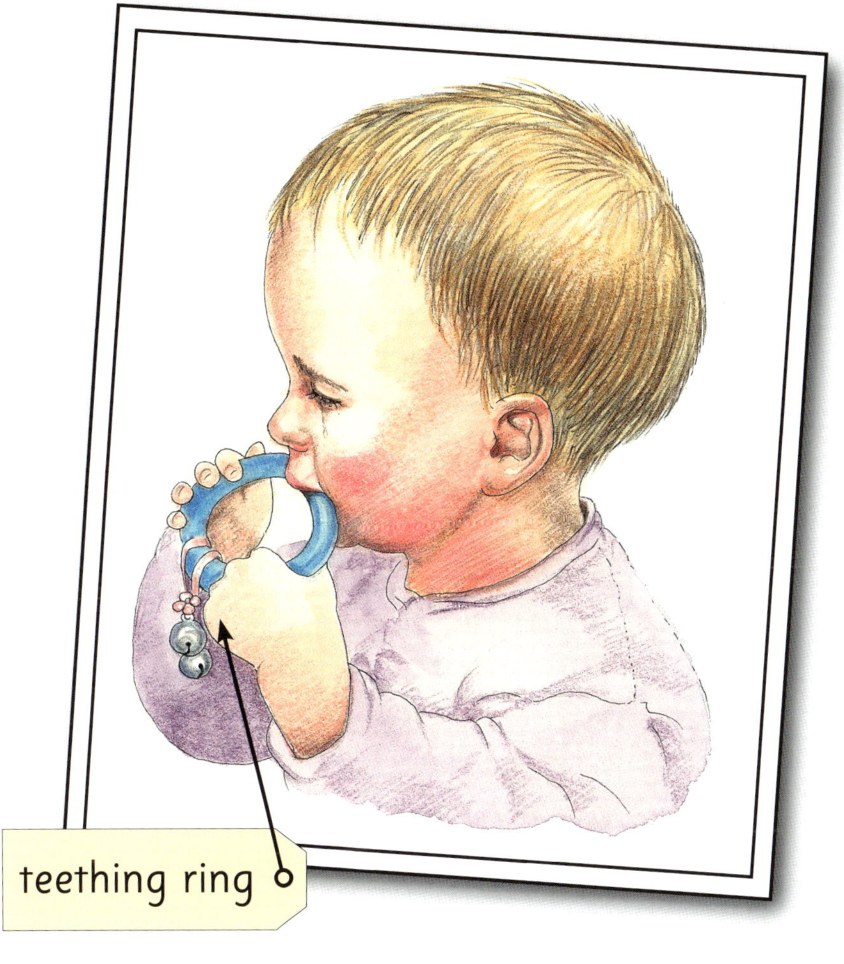

We have more than one set of teeth. As small children, we get a set of milk teeth. There are only twenty of these milk teeth. They start to wobble and fall out when we are about six or seven.

Then we get our next set of teeth. These adult teeth are much bigger and are all we get for the rest of our lives. So it is very important to keep them healthy.

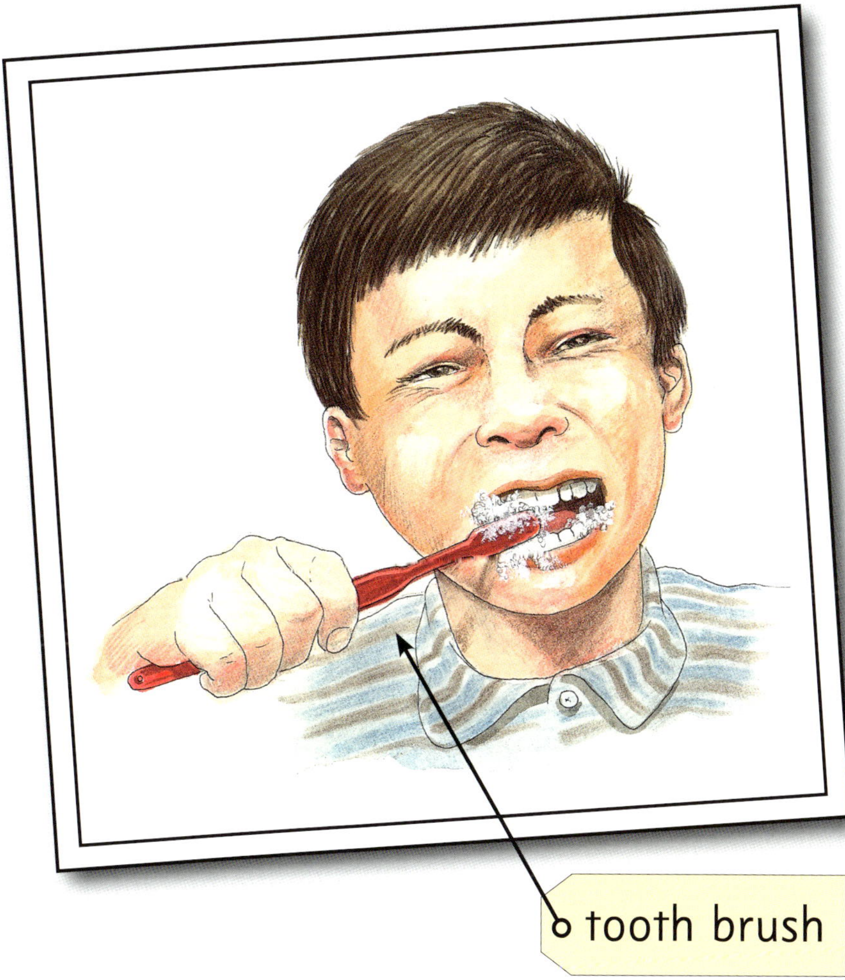

Inside the mouth, it is dark and wet. There are some living things so small that we cannot see them. They like dark and wetness, so they live and breed inside our mouths.

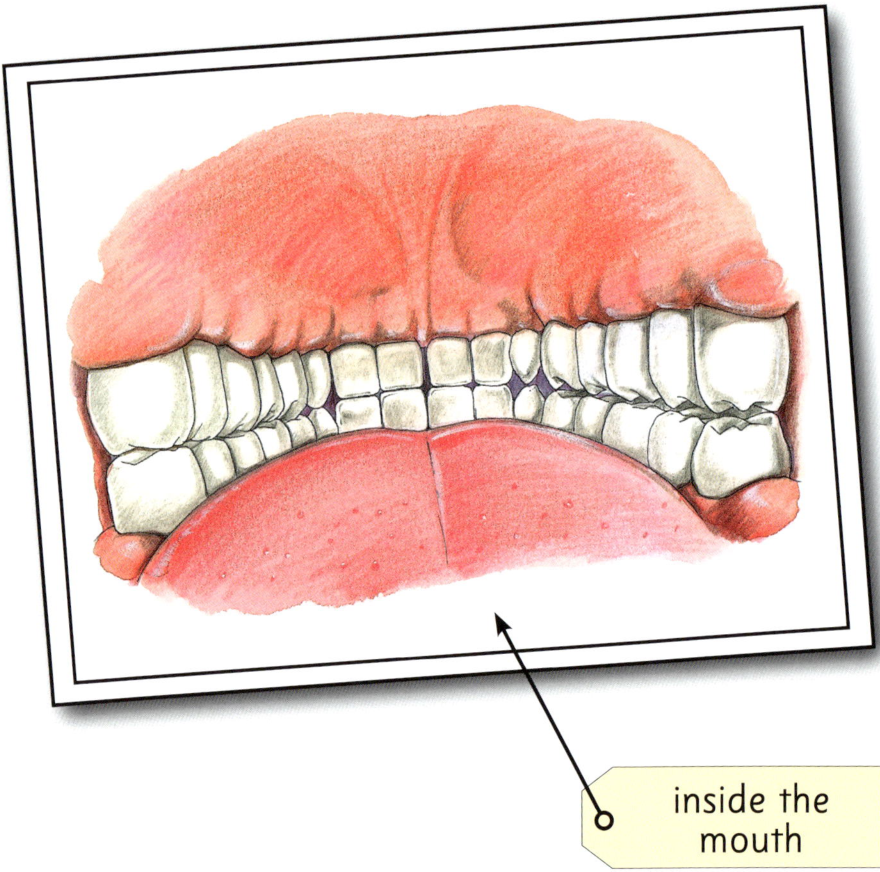

If they breed on food which has stuck to our teeth, the teeth can rot and go bad.

Brushing our teeth can help stop this happening. This is why teeth need to be brushed when you get up in the morning and before you go to bed. Brush the inside, outside, and top of the teeth.

Some food is good for teeth.

Some food is bad for teeth.

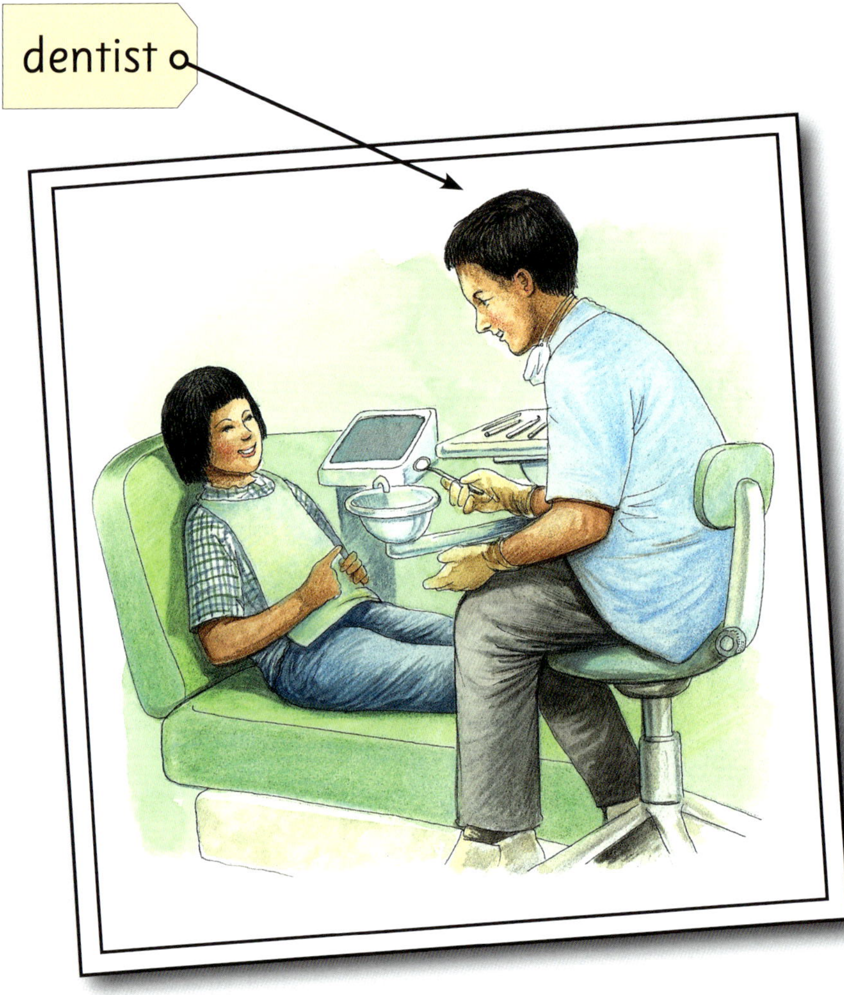

Dentists are trained to help us protect our teeth and gums. They have lots of different equipment.

Dentists have a lamp, which they shine into the mouth so they can see it better. Then they use a small mirror to help them see all the teeth. They poke around with a sort of metal toothpick, which helps them look for holes.

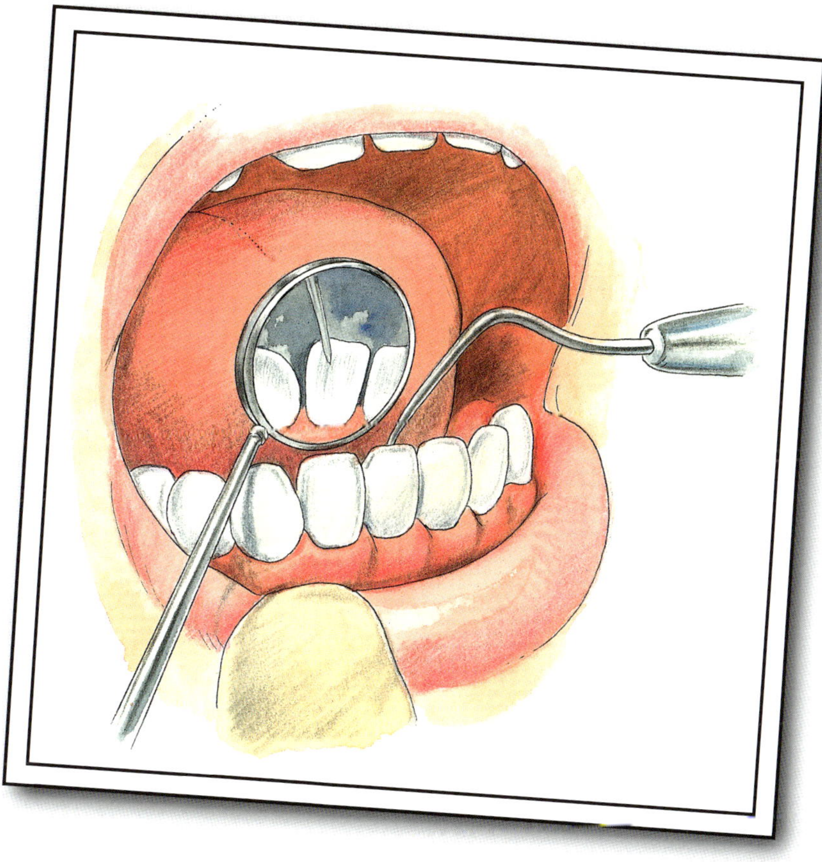

If a tooth has a hole in it, it needs a filling to stop the rot spreading. The dentist starts by injecting a painkiller into the gum to make it numb. Then the dentist drills out the rotten part of the tooth. The hole that is left is called a cavity, and this is what the dentist fills.

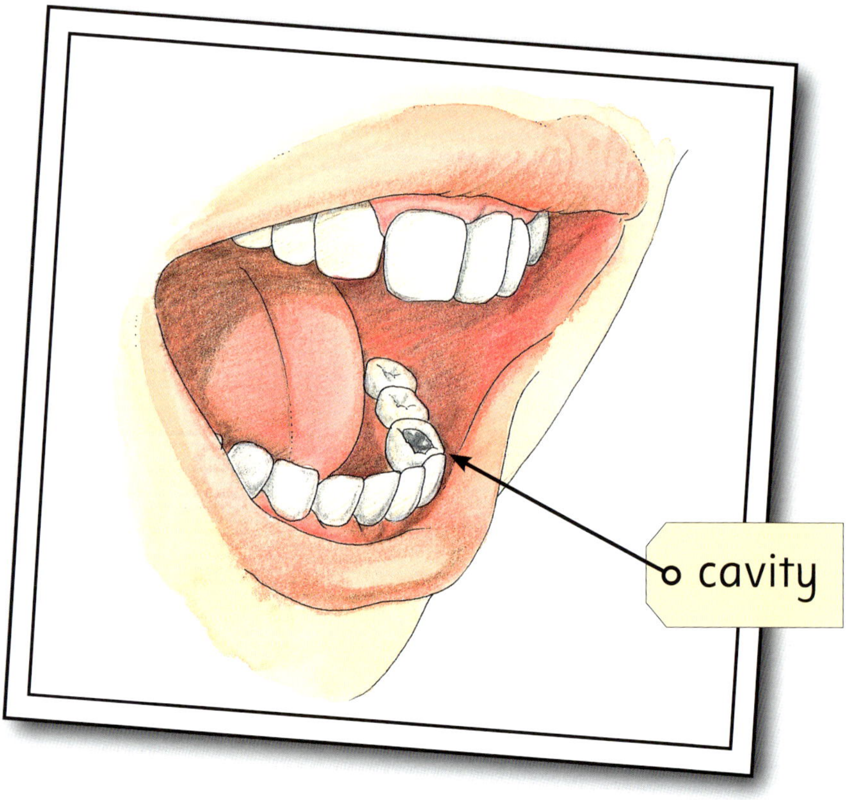

A tooth is made up of three main parts. It has a root, which joins it to the gum and to the rest of the skull. Then, on the inside, there are lots of nerves. It is the nerves which sometimes feel pain. The outside of the tooth is coated with white enamel, which is very hard.

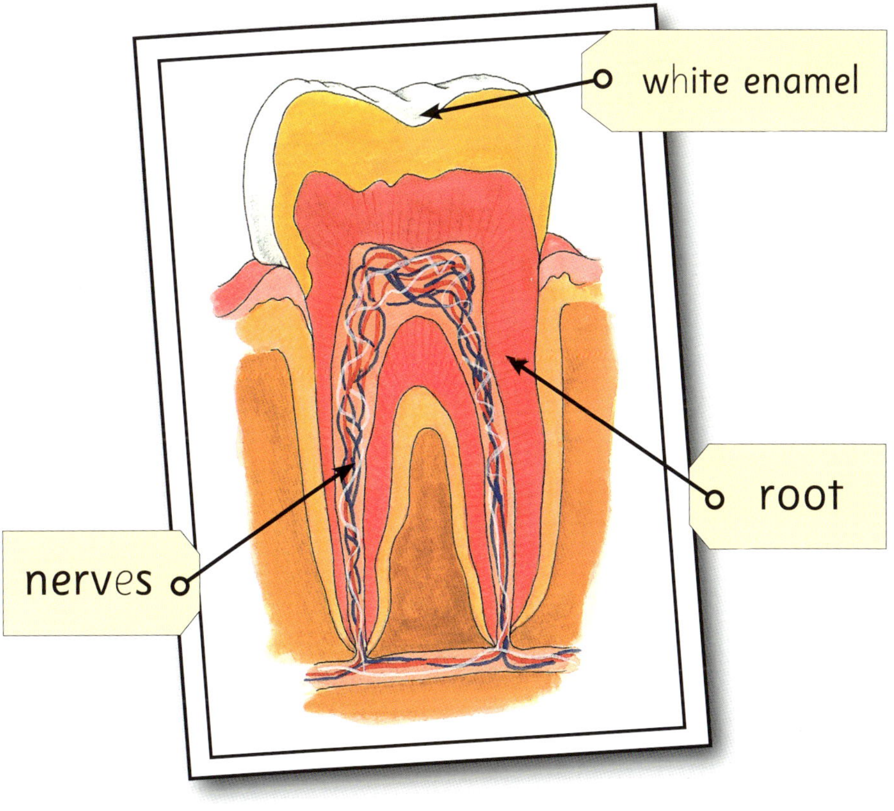

Different animals have different sorts of teeth. Animals' teeth have adapted to do all sorts of different jobs. Tusks are the biggest sort of teeth.

Animals such as rabbits, squirrels, lemmings, and muskrats have long, strong teeth. These teeth keep on getting bigger and must be used often or they will get too long. Pet rabbits sometimes have to have long teeth filed down by a vet if they have not nibbled much hard food.

Sharks have very sharp, pointed teeth. They develop teeth all the time. So if one tooth drops or falls out, they have a second one waiting to fill the gap. So sharks never run out of teeth!